Come Down to a Lower Place

YI SEOYOUNG

Translated by Janet Hong

Honford
Star

This translation first published by Honford Star 2025.

Honford Star Ltd.
Profolk, Bank Chambers
Stockport
SK1 1AR
honfordstar.com

Original Korean edition published as 낮은 곳으로 임하소서
by Alma, Inc. in 2020
Copyright © Yi Seoyoung
Translation copyright © Janet Hong 2025
All rights reserved
This translated edition is published by arrangement with Greenbook Agency.
The moral right of the translator and editors has been asserted.

ISBN (paperback): 978-1-915829-25-2
ISBN (ebook): 978-1-915829-26-9
A catalogue record for this book is available from the British Library.

Printed and bound in Paju, South Korea
Cover illustration by JaeHoon Choi
Typeset by Honford Star
Cover paper: 250 gsm Vent Nouveau by TAKEO, Japan
Endleaves: 116 gsm NT Rasha by TAKEO, Japan

This book is published with the support of the
Literature Translation Institute of Korea (LTI Korea).

1 3 5 7 9 10 8 6 4 2

SEUL PRESSED THE TOILET PAPER under her and felt a mushy, sticky substance on her fingers. Of course. A mix of disgust and anticipation filled her whenever she saw the toilet paper smeared with the familiar mucous. As always, the white discharge lay spread on the paper, accompanied by the same pungent odor. She folded the toilet paper and dropped it into the toilet.

Seul was twenty when she realized she had a problem. Her first boyfriend had noticed it. He snickered, saying he'd been scared he'd come inside her. After wiping her discharge from his crotch, he shoved the tissue right under her nose. A whiff of something sour surged up, and, startled, she pushed his hand away. He then held it to his own nose and laughed out loud.

Maybe that relationship had made her extra sensitive, but her vaginal discharge had tormented her since then. At times, her boyfriend had seemed to like it. He was happy whenever he found the whitish substance inside her, touching it with his fingers and even licking it, saying it turned him on. Sometimes, he said it looked like someone else's semen and, as a joke, called her a whore. When they ate cream pasta at a restaurant and he compared it to her vagina, Seul's heart sank. Ignoring her expression, he continued to poke fun as he stirred the pasta.

But it wasn't because of the unpleasant jokes that they broke up. They broke up because it was time. They must have shared some good memories, but whenever she thought of him, Seul felt a pain in her lower belly.

Jungyu was different. It was for that reason she chose him after several relationships. He never spoke carelessly about her body or feelings. His slightly drooping eyes always seemed to be smiling. They'd had several serious fights to the point of tears, but even in those moments, he didn't raise his voice at her. When he brought up her vaginal issues, he spoke softly.

"I'm just worried there might be a health issue. There's a bit of a smell as well ..."

A bit of a smell? Jungyu's gentle voice sounded almost plaintive. Seul could catch a whiff of herself even if she leaned forward. She felt deflated. Even though he'd cushioned his words with all sorts of padding—"Please don't take it personally," "It isn't that bad"—she couldn't help feeling miserable. But she found it difficult to even show her misery. She was more embarrassed than anything, but she didn't want to ignore Jungyu's efforts. As soon as he saw her face stiffen,

Come Down to a Lower Place

Jungyu became flustered, stammering that he'd go to the clinic with her.

"No, it's been a problem since I was young. I understand what you mean."

Seul smiled nonchalantly and stroked his head. The blanket on his bed was soft and downy, so she hurriedly put on her underwear, feeling anxious. That night, as soon as she got home, she ordered a vaginal suppository.

How young had she been when it all started? Obviously, she hadn't experienced this mushy sensation as a four- or five-year old. There had definitely been mornings when her underwear was spotless when she woke up. She remembered relieving herself while staring down at her clean panties.

When Seul was thirteen, her first period stained her underwear with a sticky brown substance that smelled like seaweed. The discharge probably hadn't started then. Was it during middle or high school? In high school, she had severe menstrual cramps and usually had to lie down in the nurse's room all morning. Initially, the nurse was concerned, but by the third month, she treated Seul as if she were faking illness every time she had her period. She hated the nurse's attitude and forced herself to sit through mornings. When she couldn't bear it any longer and fell asleep crying at her desk, she felt wronged and angry, wondering why she had to endure such pain. During breaks, her friends would pat her on the back and ask if she was okay, but their gentle strokes didn't take the pain away. Her friends told her she shouldn't take painkillers because her body would build a resistance to them.

"It's because we care about you."

Seul understood that they wanted to sound mature by using the term "resistance," but tired of enduring the pain, she started taking painkillers a day before her period began. After watching her cry every month, her mother took her to a traditional Chinese medicine clinic. The first month she took herbal medicine, the cramps vanished. Before she could tell her friends about it, her mother stopped the medicine because it was too expensive, and the cramps came back immediately.

Her discharge was no doubt related to her menstrual cramps. Gynecological conditions were like that, weren't they? But how they were related, she didn't know. The clinic didn't know what was wrong with her either. She didn't have vaginitis or an STD.

"Your vaginal discharge is just a bit excessive, that's all."

She'd gone to the gynecologist because she wanted help with her excessive discharge, but she'd paid fifty thousand won just to get an ultrasound and hear what she already knew.

Come Down to a Lower Place

As she left the clinic, her insides chafed, fueling her annoyance. Her mind buzzed with thoughts because the suppositories she had ordered had arrived the day before. She knew it was best to use them before bedtime, but she'd been too drunk to bother last night.

She made up her mind and tore open the package sitting in the entrance. Would they even work when she didn't have vaginitis or an infection? Thoughts filled her head, but one thing was clear: she wanted to put off using them. However, she couldn't just let them go to waste after paying so much for them. Just like when she didn't want to wake up in the morning, go to work, or do the dishes, she decided to get it over with and quickly removed the packaging.

Inside the package were a long applicator and some treatments. The instructions said to insert the suppository by lying down with your knees bent and curling up like a fetus. They also mentioned that after inserting the suppository, you should lie still for at least fifteen minutes. She thought about doing it on the bed, but if something leaked onto her blanket, she'd probably feel twice as bad.

She lay in front of the bathroom door and pulled down her panties. She took out the medication and placed it on the end of the applicator. Then quickly, she pushed the applicator into her vagina.

The sensation of the applicator entering her body was cold and unpleasant. She pressed the plunger. Was she supposed to stay like this for fifteen minutes? As she lay watching the time on her phone, she had several regrets. Maybe she should have done it on the bed. She should have at least put on a facial sheet mask first or inserted it after showering. As soon as fifteen minutes passed, she got up from the cold floor. The instructions said it was best to lie down for about an hour, but she didn't have that kind of luxury. While shampooing her hair, she told herself that starting tomorrow, she would shower before putting in the suppository. She had an important meeting that day.

When Seul realized she'd been assigned an important project, she was so surprised she had to check multiple times with her boss.

"Are you sure? You're sure it's that department store in the middle of Seoul?"

"Where else would Saesegae be if not in Myeongdong?" her boss said, amused. "Did you forget the layout of Seoul?"

Seul shook her hands, saying of course not, that she'd get in touch them right away. To repair the main building of Saesegae! She didn't know exactly what needed fixing, but it was an opportunity nevertheless. Even if she moved to another company, being part of such a large-scale project could add three lines to her resume. She had no plans to go to a different company anytime soon, but it was human nature to keep growing and building.

Her excitement had soared as soon as she found out about the project, and she set up a meeting right away. She had already inquired about the site of the problem area and when it could be inspected. Today, she planned to identify the problem while she was there for the meeting with the manager and secure the contract at once. On the bus to Myeongdong, all thoughts of the suppositories faded from her mind. After all, the smell of her vagina was hardly important.

Seul checked her clothes again. If she had learned anything important while working in the construction industry, it was this: wearing a suit was more professional when closing contracts, while coveralls were better for inspections. In either case, wearing high heels or heavy makeup was a no-go, as it invariably led to being asked to run coffee errands. She kept her words few but her posture straight, and she treated people comfortably but wasn't too responsive. A trustworthy expression and tone, a gaze fixed straight ahead. Although she had done this many times, thinking about Saesegae Department Store made her mouth go dry.

Though she'd reviewed the documents several times, she

took them out again. The job was simple. A smell was coming from the basement, and it could be detected on the first floor.

Naturally, it's difficult to tolerate a bad smell at home. Bad odors typically come from bathrooms or balconies with drains, causing significant stress in a space where you should be able to relax. A stench at work can even sap one's motivation. So what about department stores? Although she hadn't received the blueprints yet, the main building of Saesegae Department Store housed luxury stores. The basement showcased watches, the first floor boutiques, and the second floor designer collections.

A department store should induce you to make purchases. People buy when they're captivated, and to captivate them, they shouldn't be given time to think. Even with all these efforts, the likelihood of them not buying is still high. But if there's a stench, people won't become captivated. No matter how great the products are, it's the space that completes the product.

The department store's job is to persuade people into buying, rather than make them feel comfortable or help them work. Seul had done all kinds of repairs, but what always excited her was the task of captivating the hearts of people passing through the space. Creating a space that made them forget time and turn their attention to the next product was, essentially, magic.

Come Down to a Lower Place

There couldn't be a more ill-suited word for Saesegae Department Store than "stench." Seul gazed at the store, shining with white lights for the end of the year, and shook her head with resolve. While calling the person in charge, she pushed the door with one hand. At 10:30 a.m., the heavy glass door slid back.

She was somewhat prepared for the worst. She expected to see people grimacing as they left the store or at least wandering distractedly while they sniffed the air. If the department store sought to hire an external contractor for repairs, it meant the smell was bad enough to notice. It was the same for low-rise apartments or office spaces. If they suspected there to be a crack, the crack was usually severe, and if they said there was grime accumulating in the crevices, it was so thick that the crevices themselves had turned an entirely different color. Unless it was extremely cold or hot, people typically don't hire a company to handle everything until the situation becomes dire. As soon as Seul entered the department store, the brilliant white lights struck her eyes.

People drifted into the store and stood before products like on any other day. Seul scanned her surroundings, surprised that her sight was stimulated first, not her sense of smell. The interior was spotless, and business seemed to be bustling as usual. She glanced at the corners and crevices in the floor, but nothing caught her eye. She didn't detect an odor, although it could have been masked by other smells.

The ceiling was high, and people were milling about. Unlike the new wing, the main building seemed determined to sell the most expensive items. It was a blur of familiar brands—small and large purses, earrings that dangled like teardrops, necklaces with large beads, and hats with veils. Amid the array of colors, there was no room for a stench to interfere.

She wandered down the aisles and then changed direction, her thoughts naturally moving to a certain spot. Even if she couldn't detect a smell here, if she caught a whiff there, it meant trouble. Businesses, especially department stores, make an extra effort to eliminate odors in spaces typically suspected to smell. Seul looked up at the signs. The restroom was straight ahead on the right.

She walked past the displays of accessories, turned before a large sign, and saw the restroom illuminated by stark white lights. Her footsteps echoed in the quiet corridor. She examined the floor but didn't notice any issues. The smell was likely coming from the plumbing. Other areas might have plumbing but bathrooms always did. If the smell was coming from the restroom, it would clarify how to proceed with the repairs.

Seul opened the door to the women's restroom. The lights were bright, and the bathroom was spacious. A powder mirror covering one entire wall reflected the lights. She briefly thought back to the morning when she had inserted the suppository, recalling the awful combination of the chilly linoleum against her back and the cold applicator entering her body. She even remembered the dim kitchen lights and her impatience to get up quickly.

"This feels more like a living room than my actual living room."

Just in case, she opened the door to a stall, but as expected, she didn't notice a smell. She glanced in the direction of the men's restroom but didn't go inside. She simply wanted to grasp the situation beforehand to win over the manager. If she couldn't figure out the issue, she could always ask. Still, it was puzzling. If the smell was strong enough to reach the first floor, she should be able to find at least one troublesome spot. She was still sniffing the air when she got a call. It was ten minutes before the meeting.

"The smell comes and goes. Do you understand what I mean?"

Seul had no idea, but she couldn't say that, so she kept her mouth shut. She hoped that if she remained silent, the manager might offer more explanation, but all she did was repeat herself. She looked down at the business card she'd received.

Yurim Kim, Head of Management Team 1, Main Building.

Based on her position, Seul couldn't tell whether she had called because she was proactively pushing for repairs or because higher-ups had instructed her to do so. Seul didn't like the idea of blindly poking around without knowing the problem and then demanding more money later. There could be many causes for the smell, stemming from issues with the building itself, the people or items going in and out, or even the urban layout.

"Doesn't Saesegae have a maintenance company on contract? I would think they'd be the ones handling these issues."

The manager's face suddenly darkened. "The thing is … when we mentioned the smell, they left in the middle of the inspection."

"Pardon me?"

"They just took off. They said they couldn't do it and backed out of the contract. It was time to renew the contract anyway, so there was nothing we could do. Now we're trying to hire a company on a case-by-case basis …"

"But can they walk away from a contract like that? They should at least give you a reason."

"I know. But they weren't the only ones …" the manager said, her voice trailing off.

It seemed another company had backed out suddenly as well.

Come Down to a Lower Place

"But I didn't notice a smell at all."

"It comes and goes. Sometimes it's really overpowering, and then it completely disappears. Another company said they couldn't fix it during the inspection. We hadn't even paid the contract fee yet, so there wasn't anything we could do when they left."

"I came a bit early to have a look. I checked the restroom and floors on the first floor, but I didn't smell anything. If there's a particular area where the smell is stronger, please let me know."

The manager's eyes widened. "Does that mean you'll take the job?"

"We need to do an inspection first to see if we can resolve the issue and then give you an estimate."

"Yes, of course! Please take a look. There's no smell today, but there might be tomorrow."

"So where exactly is it coming from?"

"When it does smell, it comes from the basement up to the first floor. But when it doesn't, there's no smell at all."

That seemed impossible.

"Regardless of whether we take the job or not, you'll still need to pay for the inspection."

The sewage treatment facility used a contact aeration system, a common method in urban areas. This involved adding air into the water to promote decomposition, which quickly reduced carbon dioxide and made smells fade faster. While it wasn't the most environmentally friendly approach, it was practical and suitable for cities. In any case, it shouldn't have caused any odors.

Building repairs had been recorded since 2002, with the only modifications after that being to the septic tank and some remodeling. Back in her office, Seul reviewed the documents she'd been given and then pulled out Manager Kim's business card. Businesses that work with long-term contractors often don't know how much information to provide. She fiddled with the usage approval record on top of the modification records. October 24, 1930. The capacity remained the same before and after the remodeling: "13,000 people." In 1930, Seoul's population was less than 400,000. Building a structure that could accommodate more than 3% of the city's population back then showed the ambition of the builder.

She noticed a change in the manager's voice when she answered the phone. With an awkward laugh, Yurim Kim spoke slowly, making no effort to hide her discomfort. It was clear she wanted her unease to be noticed.

"Now, why would you need to see the old records for the inspection?"

Come Down to a Lower Place

"If I know whether this issue existed before, it makes it easier to understand the problem."

"Can't you just do the inspection first?"

"So you're okay with closing down the store and digging up the floors for a few months?"

"Oh, it can't take that long ... Maybe two weeks at the most?"

"If the problem has to be fixed in two weeks, we have to know as much as possible before we start. It's not like I have some superpower where I can just press a button to figure out what's wrong."

Four hours had passed before Yurim Kim called back.

"They said you can't scan or fax the old records. I think it's best if you come back here and take a look. When can you come?"

Seul left her office, grumbling about being told to come and go in this cold weather without even a hint of an apology. Outside, the winter sky was refreshingly clear for the first time in a while, crisp in a way that was different from the autumn sky. The air was so dry that the sunlight felt as sharp as ice. On the way to the bus stop, she heard music mixed with the sound of bells—a fitting sound for winter. Listening to the Christmas carols from a pastry stall right behind the bus stop, she curled her body and then stretched. The dry air made it seem unlikely they would have a white Christmas. As she thought about not being able to buy a car again this winter, a thought struck her: *I wonder why they didn't build a parking lot?*

The new wing of Saesegae had a parking lot that went down six levels, but the main building had only two indoor stalls. A new parking lot hadn't been built during the renovation. She had never considered that a large department store might not have underground parking. On the way to the new wing, Seul mentally reviewed all the department stores she knew.

In the office at the new wing, Manager Kim brought several documents under the strict condition that they must not be copied or photographed. Some of the papers looked so old and brittle they seemed like they might crumble upon contact. One of the documents was dated eighty-four years ago. Seul carefully held the paper by its edges and skimmed the text. As expected of an old document, it was filled with Chinese characters that she could barely make out. She slowly started reading from the top.

The manager brought some green tea in a paper cup and hurried out of the office, saying she had to use the restroom. Judging by her quick steps, she must have been in quite a rush. As soon as she left, Seul pulled out her cellphone. She felt like

Come Down to a Lower Place

she was in a scene from *Mission Impossible*. When Yurim Kim returned, she quickly gathered up the documents, as if realizing her mistake of leaving Seul alone with them.

"Did you find anything useful?"

"Yes, it seems there was an issue with the smell back then too. The malodor was so bad they had to reinforce the floor."

"Malodor?"

"The stench."

"Oh, so they worked on the floor back then?"

"Yes."

"Then maybe you can do the same thing this time."

After parting with the manager on a friendly note, Seul returned to the office and opened the photos she had taken on her phone. Handling construction documents with such secrecy usually implied something serious, like a death, financial irregularities, or hidden slush funds. Was she about to uncover some secret funds from a big company? If so, she should probably alert the media instead of taking the job. But it was unlikely that any slush funds from the Japanese colonial period would still be around. Could gold bars be hidden under the floor? Feeling like a detective, she carefully read each Chinese character. Despite her limited proficiency, the explanation she'd given Manager Kim earlier turned out to be correct.

"The malodor (臭味) rising up was so severe that the work (工事) of reinforcing (厚) the floor surface (床面) had to be carried out (試行)."

This meant the floor was thickened to combat the smell.

"Worker Kim (金) Gaebong removed the floor and went down, but upon emerging, he strongly advised against entering.

"Upon following Kim (金) Gaebong down, Jungbon (中本) had a seizure (発作) on the spot and was transferred (移送) to Severance Hospital, formerly Jejungwon (濟衆院)."

Even after reading the whole document, it was still unclear what lay beneath the floor. At the end, there was a hastily scrawled note. The earlier text was written with a fine brush, but this part looked like it was done with an ink pen—small, hurried letters with crooked lines.

"After that day, Gaebong fell ill for three days and eventually lost his mind. 牝汚災, 牝汚災."

She could easily read the second character, 汚 (o) for filth, and 災 (jae) for disaster, but she didn't recognize the first character, 牝. She opened an online dictionary and traced the character crookedly with her mouse. It was "bin," the character for "female." Bin-o-jae. Female, filth, disaster. She didn't know exactly what the phrase meant, but it suggested they wouldn't find out what was under the floor unless they

Come Down to a Lower Place

tore it up. When Seul called and suggested removing the floor, Manager Kim balked.

"No, absolutely not. You need to find another way."

"But the smell's coming from the floor. How are we supposed to figure out what's wrong without removing it?"

"They made the floor thicker in the past, didn't they? Can't you just do the same this time?"

"To make it thicker, we'd still need to remove the marble layer and then add more on top."

"Hold on, I'll explain in an email."

About three hours later, Seul got an email from Manager Kim saying that only the marble could be removed and that no one was permitted to go below it. The contract contained a clause prohibiting digging below the marble, which was also specified in the task order. Additionally, another clause stated that if they dug deeper and any issues arose, they wouldn't be paid the remaining balance and would be responsible for covering any damages.

Seul wondered if there really was gold hidden underground but decided to let it go. She didn't really care what was down there. What mattered was that she needed to find a material that could block the smell without removing the entire flooring, but she had no idea what that could be.

Once she agreed to the department store's conditions, the inspection request was easily accepted. Although she wanted to inspect the basement floor when there were no customers around, due to the visit of an important guest the next day and the complexity of the security system, she was granted only a quick look. She would have to wait until after construction began to do any detailed measuring and examination.

What bothered her was that not once during the contract negotiations did she catch a whiff of anything foul. Honestly, removing the marble and adding another layer wasn't difficult. It would bring in money and add to her experience, but there was no guarantee that the smell wouldn't come back. The purpose of construction is to solve a fundamental problem, not to apply a temporary fix. If she wanted a quick fix, there were plenty of other methods.

For Seul, the biggest appeal of construction work was that she could fix the root cause of a problem. When she was a girl tormented by menstrual cramps, Seul would hunch over her desk and imagine removing her uterus, splitting it down the middle, and drying it in the sun. If there were any cysts inside, she would carefully pop and remove each one, apply ointment, sew the freshly dried uterus together, and put it back into her body. Somehow, imagining this lessened the pain. But of course, that was impossible.

Come Down to a Lower Place

But construction was different. There's a reason for every bad smell. It could be a broken pipe from rust, a decayed wall, or a dead pigeon in the septic tank. But instead of examining these potential issues, they just wanted her to remove the top layer and cover it with something thicker. Seul couldn't help but feel like she was deceiving them. Right then, she heard a squelch under her feet.

A squelch in the corner of the marble floor and in a department store? It didn't make any sense.

She'd turned into a dark corner and stepped on a puddle of clear slime that was slightly smaller than the size of her palm. She couldn't figure out where the liquid had come from. It must have seeped up from the floor. This was the spot. She quickly scanned her surroundings, snapped a few photos, and jotted down some notes. If they focused on this area, they might be able to solve the problem without digging deep.

As soon as she tried to step toward the corner, a uniformed employee appeared. Looking startled, he rushed over.

"Excuse me, ma'am, is there something wrong?"

"Oh, am I not allowed here?"

"No, no. There are only staff restrooms here. Customer restrooms are on the opposite side."

Separate restrooms for customers and staff? Now that she thought about it, she'd never come across any staff members in the restroom. She peered past the employee into the dark. No bright lights or signs indicated a restroom. Were there lights further in? As soon as she heard the word "restroom," she suddenly felt the urge to go. She knew this wasn't a real urge, but she couldn't just ignore it either. When she tried to head toward the restroom, the employee blocked her way.

"Ma'am, the restrooms here are for employees only. Customer restrooms are on the other side."

Seul was about to explain that she was overseeing the repairs, but she saw the employee's name tag and decided to keep quiet. Next to his name was the title "Temporary Associate." Mentioning the smell and repairs to a temporary worker could create a bigger problem. Not that temps would be held responsible for any issues anyway. Seul nodded and quickly headed the other way.

The bathroom floor was cleaner than her home. Under the bright lights, she frantically raised the toilet lid. The seat was warm, like one with an electronic bidet function. On the closed stall door was the phrase: "A beautiful you leaves a beautiful loo." She didn't see a trash bin, just a disposal for sanitary napkins. She let out a quiet trickle. She focused, squeezing out every last bit. A thinner stream trickled out, and at the same time, a sharp pain shot up her urethra. She bowed her head, enduring the pain.

Come Down to a Lower Place

A urinary tract infection again. The stress of landing this project must have triggered it. She had experienced it countless times. Even on the day of her college entrance exam, she'd had to go to the bathroom multiple times because of a UTI. In the end, she'd resorted to using a sanitary pad, holding out until the pain was unbearable. It was a frustrating, chronic condition. She'd rush to the restroom as if her bladder was about to burst, only to let out a ridiculously small amount of urine, hardly enough for a urine test, and this would be followed by excruciating pain. She couldn't fully relieve herself, nor could she hold it in.

After researching UTIs, Seul had learned the condition was more common in women than in men due to their shorter urethras and anatomical differences, which made it easier for infections to reach the bladder. As she sat on the toilet enduring the pain, she felt resentful of people who had no idea what this kind of suffering was like.

She stared blankly at the closed door, waiting for the pain to subside while the familiar, fishy stink and the odor of urine pierced her nostrils. Every time she bent her knees, she caught a whiff of herself. It had been three days since she started using the suppositories, but they didn't seem to be working. They weren't cheap either.

She hadn't seen Jungyu since beginning the treatment.

She had texted him about possibly taking on a new project but hadn't given any details. She wanted to tell him in person, but work was busy, and Jungyu seemed tired, so she hadn't suggested meeting up. With the end of the year approaching, they'd probably go on a date before Christmas, and she could talk to him then. The thought of telling him she was in charge of repairing such a big building made her proud.

She took some toilet paper and wiped, noticing a bit of blood mixed with the urine. It wasn't her period. From her experience, when there was blood, the infection lasted much longer. She heaved a deep sigh and pulled up her pants. On her way out of the restroom, she called Manager Kim.

"I was wondering, as long as we stick to the contract terms, everything else is fine, right?"

"Yes, but why do you ask?"

"I wanted to take a look at the drainpipes."

"Oh, they're buried underground ..."

"No, not those. The ones in the bathrooms above ground."

"The bathrooms?"

"Yes, I saw the customer bathrooms, but I noticed there are separate bathrooms for staff."

"Oh, right. Staff bathrooms are on specific floors."

"I'd like to check both. Besides, I noticed something odd in the basement earlier."

Come Down to a Lower Place

"Something odd?"

"I'll include it in my report later. But I'd first like to inspect the drainage facilities."

"Ah ... then you should go with one of our maintenance staff."

Early the next morning, a young man who looked like he'd just finished his military service met Seul.

"I was told you inspected the customer restrooms already. But if you need to see the staff restrooms, we'll have to go together. They're only on the basement, third, and sixth floors."

His face clearly showed his reluctance to accompany her.

"Let's start with the men's customer bathrooms, then the staff's. I can inspect the women's customer bathrooms on my own ... but are you sure that would be all right?"

"You said you could do it alone. Why are you asking me?"

Seul noticed the name tag on his vest—"Lee Minhwan, Temporary Associate." He handed her a vest.

"Put this on. People get surprised if you're not wearing it."

They decided to start on the sixth floor. He went inside the men's customer bathroom first. "Drainage inspection!"

He came out and shrugged. "I think it's empty, but I yelled just in case someone's on the toilet. You can go in now."

The men's bathroom was just as clean as the others, and

she didn't detect an odor either. There were no leaks or cracks, not even the slightest sign of water damage. The walls were spotless, and the grout lines were pristine. If anything, it was unusual how all the bathrooms looked cleaner than her own bedroom, and they all smelled the same too, as though they used the same air freshener. It was almost unbelievable there was running water, for every spot was completely dry. Did they clean the bathrooms every few hours?

From the sixth floor down to the first, the worker stared at his phone the entire time, not saying anything. Unable to bear the awkward silence any longer, she smiled and tried to make conversation.

"You seem busy."

"Not at all."

"I see …"

A long silence resumed. Occasionally, they encountered men at the urinals, but the maintenance vest acted like an invisibility cloak. Seeing the vest, the men continued with their business, washing their hands and leaving without a second glance. In the men's bathroom on the basement floor, one man continued to fiddle with his new watch even after seeing Seul step inside.

"You wanted to check the staff bathrooms next, right? They're this way," the worker said.

Come Down to a Lower Place

"They must think I'm a maintenance worker when I wear this vest. They don't even care that I'm a woman."

"Pretty much."

Seul laughed awkwardly again. Meanwhile, her UTI was flaring up, and she followed the worker, knees pressed together. As soon as they reached the bathroom, Seul practically sprinted inside and sat down on the toilet. Only then did she realize how dim this bathroom was compared to the others. As always, hardly any urine came out. After a short bout of pain, she emerged from the stall, noticing the sink area was a lot brighter. Another worker was there, washing her hands. As Seul approached, she flinched in surprise. Blood was running down the worker's hands.

"Oh, you're bleeding," she blurted out.

At Seul's sharp cry, the woman glanced up. Seul shifted her gaze to the woman's face. It was pale, almost ghostly, and the makeup under her eyes was caked on, as if she had applied several layers of concealer. The bright lights highlighted every detail of her skin, including her baby hairs. The worker resumed washing her hands, unfazed.

Feeling uneasy at her calm expression, Seul looked down at the sink. The worker's hands were now clean, as if the blood had only been in her imagination. Seul had assumed she was injured, but it seemed there was no injury. Yet there had been so much blood … Suddenly, she realized the woman might be menstruating. She finished washing her hands and left the bathroom, drying them on her skirt. Seul felt embarrassed, realizing she had made a scene over someone's period.

She quickly washed her hands and noticed a reflective plate at the bottom of the mirror. It was engraved with the words: "Employees who have wept must check their faces before returning to work."

If the sink areas in the staff bathrooms were extra bright for this reason, it seemed excessive. She gazed at the words with a bitter smile and stepped out of the bathroom.

"You were in there for a while."

"I had to use the bathroom too."

"Ah, no wonder you ran in there."

On their way up to the staff bathrooms on the third floor, Seul saw the worker who had been washing blood off her hands. She was standing in the luxury accessories department on the first floor.

"What took you so long?" another worker asked.

"I've been having issues every time I go to the bathroom. I haven't been feeling well."

"Do you have a bladder infection? I have it too."

When a customer stopped to look at earrings, the pale

worker quickly hurried over and stood in front of them. A bright smile, completely different from the face Seul had seen in the bathroom, spread across her face. Seul walked by slowly, looking at the earrings from the other side, but no one paid any attention to her. It must be because she was wearing the maintenance vest. She glanced down at the left of her chest and saw that her vest had no name tag.

Manager Kim had said that any construction work should be announced at least two weeks in advance. The very next day, a small notice was posted in the lobby, stating that the basement floor would be renovated over the next two weeks. It also added that the first through sixth floors would be operating as usual, so there was no need to worry.

"How do you know we'll be able to finish in two weeks?" Seul asked Manager Kim later.

"It's got to be done in two weeks," Manager Kim replied.

"And what do you plan to do about the construction noise?"

"Well, we can't do anything about that. But please try to minimize the noise and carry out the construction outside business hours as much as possible. Can you soundproof the ceiling somehow? I've heard there are noise-canceling foam panels these days."

"We'll try. By the way, what do you mean by renovation? What we're doing is repairs."

"If we call it 'repairs,' customers might think there's something wrong with the building and get worried."

But there is *something wrong,* Seul grumbled to herself. However, she didn't want to argue with a client. She needed to finish this project well and move on to the next one. Suddenly, she thought of Jungyu's clean, fluffy blanket. If she could get a good night's rest under that blanket with him, she felt she'd have the energy to tackle everything.

After clearing out all the display areas, she pried up one of the floor tiles. The marble was thick, and underneath, the concrete was rock-solid. Thickening the concrete was an option, as long as lowering the ceiling wasn't an issue.

While inspecting the basement, Seul found the spot where the mysterious slime had been oozing out. Although the slime was gone, she spray-painted a large sign to mark the spot. To eliminate the odor for good, they needed to address the root cause. Ideally, exposing it to oxygen and letting it oxidize would be the best solution, but they decided to dig first to see if that was possible. If not, they could always cover it back up—just like they'd done back in the 1930s.

She needed to plan for both scenarios: one where they could fix the problem by digging up the floor, and another where that wouldn't work. Lost in thought, she walked out the back of the department store when she felt someone watching her. An elderly man was staring—no, glaring—at her. He looked like he was in his late seventies or eighties, definitely not young. His sunken cheeks made his hostile eyes stand out even more. Though his clothes were worn and faded, he looked neat—hardly like someone who was mentally unstable. She gave him a quick glance before looking away. It was best to avoid people like that. Things could get messy, especially if he'd been drinking. She didn't see anything in his hands, but ever since she'd been hit with a cane by a drunken old man on the street, she'd been wary of elderly men. As she quickened her pace, the old man suddenly started running after her.

"Don't do it!"

When he charged toward her, shouting, she broke into a run. But the old man was faster than she'd expected—shockingly fast for someone so old with white hair. Where did he get all that strength? The faster he ran, the more panicked she became. She was gasping for breath, but something told her she shouldn't stop. More than anything, she was terrified.

She sprinted toward the main road, thinking that if there were more people around, someone was more likely to help her. But on the main road, the old man seemed to move even faster. Where was the police station? There had to be one nearby. While frantically scanning the area, she nearly tripped. The old man shouted again.

"Stop digging!

His voice was deep and eerie, and it seemed to shake the ground. It clawed at Seul's ears like a rake. She screamed and bolted—not toward the police station, but to the bus stop.

The old man kept shouting as he chased her. "Stop digging! You have to stop! Or you'll unleash the curse! You'll unleash the curse of Bin-o-jae!"

Just in time, she jumped onto the first bus she saw. The old man ran after her, but the bus door closed before he could get on. He pounded on the door, but the bus took off without him. She barely managed to stand, clutching a pole, while the driver glanced at her worriedly through the rearview mirror.

"Miss, are you okay?"

"Yes …"

Her legs started to shake uncontrollably, and she collapsed into an empty seat. Tears streamed down her face.

That night, she woke up three times, each time to the old man's cry: "You'll unleash the curse of Bin-o-jae!"

In her dream, the old man stood in a gaping, blood-red hole, in the middle of the department store, shouting that the curse was being released. As he raised his hands, the ground beneath Seul crumbled. She jolted awake to find it was 2:32 a.m.

Bin-o-jae. Where had she heard that name before?

Come Down to a Lower Place

Bin-o-jae … It was from that document where she'd struggled to read the first character and had to look it up in the dictionary. "Bin" had meant "female." That's all she could remember—nothing else in the document stuck with her. Why had that word been mentioned? It hadn't seemed important at the time.

After lying awake for the rest of the night, Seul arrived at work half an hour earlier than usual. She often arrived about twenty minutes early, but today, the office was completely quiet. It was the first time she'd arrived before everyone else in her department since starting the job. As soon as she got there, she searched for the photos she had saved. When she zoomed in, she saw the words: "After that day, Gaebong fell ill for three days and eventually lost his mind. Bin-o-jae, Bin-o-jae."

This information didn't have anything to do with the project. She must have considered it so unimportant that she'd read it, filed it away, and forgotten all about it, along with the details about Kim Gaebong, who'd worked on the project, and a Japanese man by the name of Jungbon. When she looked closer, she noticed smaller text beneath the characters for "Bin-o-jae" that she hadn't seen before. The text was so tiny that she had to press the control key and zoom in even further to read it.

"A grudge flowing from between the legs lies deep underground, so this grudge must never be released."

Huh? It still seemed completely unrelated to the construction project. With nothing resolved, Seul closed the image and headed to the break room for some coffee.

On the day construction began, Seul gave the workers a brief explanation along with some instructions.

"Basically, we're going to pour a thick, new layer of concrete over the old one. But since this repair is about the smell, we'll start by checking the area circled in red to see what's underneath. We'll drill down and see if it's something we can fix. If not, we'll just pour the new concrete over it. If nothing comes up when we drill, we'll go ahead with the pouring. Got it?"

The workers nodded.

"So, should we report back after we've drilled through the circle?"

"Yes. It shouldn't take long, right?"

"We'll have to see how thick it is, but we should be able to drill through it in three days, tops."

"All right, let's get started then!"

She clapped her hands, and the drills started to whirr. As the noise buzzed in the background, she quickly responded to Jungyu's text about meeting this Thursday evening. It

Come Down to a Lower Place

wasn't that she'd been avoiding him, but with the construction and the whole Bin-o-jae situation, she hadn't spoken to him in the past few days.

As she typed, she sensed that something was off, and her attention drifted down to her crotch. She couldn't tell if she was just being paranoid or if there really was a smell coming from between her legs. It had been nearly two weeks since she'd started using the suppository, and she had hoped it would start working by now.

The next morning, as usual, Seul took out the suppository, but this time she realized the smell wasn't just in her head. Without warning, her period had started. She quickly grabbed some painkillers instead and took them. Then, not long after arriving at work, she was told that the department store was having a company dinner Thursday evening.

"All right, we'll make sure our team attends as well," she replied.

She tapped her fingers on the desk for a moment before texting Jungyu: *Sorry, but I can't meet this Thursday evening after all.*

The venue for the company dinner was a high-end barbecue restaurant with high ceilings. Well, it was Saesegae Department Store, so that was expected. As Seul watched her team eagerly scanning the menu, she felt like the dinner might not be so bad after all. The assorted prime Korean beef was 74,000 won per person, and even if the company didn't go for that, the New Zealand ribs were 44,000 won. She figured they would be treated to something like that at least.

Until now, she had only dealt with Manager Kim, but now, a man she was meeting for the first time smiled warmly as he handed her his business card.

"I should have introduced myself sooner. It's great to finally meet you. I'm Ha Jaehong."

Seul also handed him her card and bowed. Mr. Ha made some polite small talk, stressing the importance of giving customers a comfortable shopping experience and adding that it was frustrating to see the same issues keep coming up. He thanked her in advance for her hard work, then took a seat at the center of the reserved table in the farthest corner. When her team members sat at the opposite end, he asked why they were sitting so far away without bothering to get up.

"Team Leader, why don't you sit over here?"

Seul took a seat diagonally across from Mr. Ha while glancing around for Manager Kim. She spotted her sitting at the far end of the table, avoiding eye contact with Mr. Ha. Seul let out a quiet sigh, careful not to let Mr. Ha hear.

"Five large orders of the spicy squid and pork belly, please!" Mr. Ha said, placing the order in a loud voice.

Come Down to a Lower Place

Seul looked at him, startled he'd ordered one of the cheaper items on the menu, but he just chuckled.

"You see, this place is famous for its spicy squid and pork belly."

A group of people arrived a little late and sat down. Mr. Ha suddenly stood up and waved them over.

"I invited some of the first-floor staff who could make it. You'll probably run into them during the repairs."

Those who sat down didn't look particularly cheerful, and Seul understood why. Who actually wanted to go to a company dinner? The latecomers hesitated before taking the empty seats between her and the other team members. The woman who sat next to Seul looked vaguely familiar. As Seul studied her face, she realized it was the employee from the accessories department she had seen in the staff restroom, the one washing blood off her hands. The woman, looking glum, stared down at the plate in front of her. Recognizing her, Seul blurted, "Hello!"

She glanced at Seul, just as she had in the restroom, then picked up her chopsticks and grabbed some kimchi. Instead of replying, she crunched on the kimchi. As Seul awkwardly tried to brush off the snub, large pans of spicy squid and pork belly were placed on each table. As the chili sauce boiled, a savory aroma quickly spread through the air. Seeing Seul get snubbed, the woman across the table spoke up.

"We work at the Rankip & Adell store on the first floor."

She had been there that day as well. She was the one who'd mentioned she also had a bladder infection. She didn't recognize Seul, probably because Seul had been wearing her staff vest. It made sense that the person next to her didn't remember her either. She smiled and continued speaking.

"Dahan's just saving her energy right now. We get so tired smiling all day at the store that by the time I get home, I'm completely wiped out. But Dahan's great at pacing herself. She smiles when she needs to and holds back when she doesn't. Isn't that right, Dahan?"

Dahan just glanced at the woman without responding. Mr. Ha jumped in.

"Dahan is pretty famous on our side too. She's the queen of sales. I'm not in the same department, but I happened to check the records once and wow …" Mr. Ha said, giving her a thumbs-up.

"Not sure when you checked, but last month …" the woman across the table whispered into Mr. Ha's ear.

Mr. Ha's eyebrows shot up. "Really? Is that true? What's your secret? Let's have a toast! Employees like Dahan are the reason we say, 'When our people succeed, we succeed.' How do you do it? Come on, everyone, fill up your glasses!"

As people quickly poured water or soju into their glasses, Dahan quietly chewed on a piece of squid, her face pale.

Come Down to a Lower Place

Clearly excited, Mr. Ha leaned over and filled Dahan's glass with soju himself. "Dahan, if you don't want to drink, just raise your glass with us."

But Dahan didn't look up or lift her glass. The woman next to Mr. Ha gave him a little nudge, a gesture even Seul noticed. "Dahan's not into this sort of thing."

"Oh … is that right?"

"Yes, maybe we should just toast on our own."

As if feeling a little awkward, Mr. Ha quickly raised his glass. "To the partnership between Yukwang Construction and our main office, and to our mutual success!"

"To our success!"

Everyone downed their shots in one go. It tasted sweet, likely from the sugar content. Noticing Seul's empty glass, the woman across from her quickly refilled it.

"Oh, it looks like you can handle your liquor. Are you the one overseeing the repairs?"

"Yes, I am." Seul quickly dug into her bag and handed over a business card.

"Lee Seul? What a lovely name, just like the way you handled that drink."

The woman gave the soju bottle a light shake. Joking about Seul's ability to drink was common at these gatherings. Seul nodded and smiled.

"I don't have my business cards with me right now, but I'm Yoon Seonghui. I'm the manager of Rankip & Adell. And this is Jung Dahan. I heard the area with the worst smell is right below our store. It's not an easy issue to bring up with the head office, so we're really grateful they're taking care of it. The smell isn't always bad, but sometimes it's really strong. I hope you can resolve it for us."

Seul smiled politely and reached for more spicy pork belly when she felt her phone vibrate on her thigh. Glancing down, she saw a message from Jungyu. *Miss you. Can you come over after the dinner?*

A smile spread across her face before she even realized it, as if her facial muscles had a mind of their own, but the urge to pee struck again, and her happiness quickly faded. Dealing with both a period and a bladder infection was tough. She grabbed her pouch from her bag and headed to the restroom. As she stepped into a stall, she quickly texted back: *I'll come over as soon as dinner's over.*

The smell of blood hit her as soon as she pulled down her underwear, masking the other smell she'd been worried about. Well, since she was on her period, there would be no need take off her underwear later. She quickly changed her pad.

Come Down to a Lower Place

When she returned to her seat, the others were discussing something she knew nothing about. Since she was separated from her team, she focused on the food in front of her. Dahan, sitting next to her, did the same. Watching Dahan's slow, deliberate movements, Seul felt a bit envious. It seemed Dahan could get away with being rude because she brought in strong sales. The conversation across the table was about someone Seul didn't know.

"I heard she had surgery recently."

"Yes, she went through several rounds of IVF."

"Oh my gosh, I've heard that's really tough."

"Exactly. And after all that …"

"What happened?"

"One day, she noticed something weird about her period."

"About her cycle?"

"No, the blood. It was different—something seemed off."

"What? How can the blood be different?"

"I don't get it either."

Mr. Ha, who'd been facing the other way while talking, suddenly whipped around.

"Hey, can we not talk about periods and blood while we're eating? It's disgusting. It's the same as talking about bodily waste!"

The conversation stopped abruptly. In the awkward silence that followed, Seul suddenly thought of the term "Bin-o-jae."

Female, filth, disaster. Could it be related to menstruation? As she pondered its meaning, the word slipped out of her mouth.

"Bin-o-jae ..."

Dahan looked up at Seul for the first time that evening. Startled by the sudden attention, Seul stared back at her. Dahan leaned in, her eyes wide.

"What did you just say?"

"Pardon?"

"So you know? If your period doesn't come on time and the blood overflows, it'll awaken the power of Bin-o-jae."

"Period? Blood?"

Dahan's face was uncomfortably close, making Seul uneasy. From this proximity, the dark circles under Dahan's eyes looked even darker, and her face seemed chapped. Feeling a little threatened, Seul leaned back. Just then, Dahan grabbed her bag and stood up.

"I'm leaving now."

Seul relaxed and placed her bag on Dahan's empty seat. The dinner was winding down, and they'd finished most of the food. As she chewed on a piece of pork belly, she kept repeating the words in her mind: period, menstruation, Bin-o-jae, female ... What did it mean for blood to overflow if your period didn't come on time?

Come Down to a Lower Place

Once, while swimming in the sea, she had kept a tampon in too long, and blood started leaking down her legs. She had to quickly wrap a friend's shirt around herself and run to the changing room. If you don't take care of the blood, it overflows. Since that day, she had been too anxious to use tampons.

When she arrived at Jungyu's place, he was slightly flushed. "I had a few drinks with friends since you were at your company dinner."

Seul took off her coat and hung it on the rack before sitting next to Jungyu, who was leaning against the bed. "I wanted to have another drink with you, but I guess not tonight."

"You know I'm a lightweight."

One of the things she liked about Jungyu was his low tolerance for alcohol. He didn't particularly enjoy drinking and never drank to the point of passing out. It seemed he didn't like the feeling of getting buzzed. He was the kind of guy who was content having just one or two beers with Seul. Life felt much more stable with someone who didn't have issues with drinking.

Jungyu took out the T-shirt and sweatpants she usually wore when she stayed over. While she changed, Jungyu slipped under the covers.

"Are you tired?"

"Are you kidding? I'm wide awake."

As soon as she joined him under the covers, Jungyu eagerly lifted her shirt. She gently pushed his head away.

"I'm on my period."

"Really?"

Jungyu stared at the ceiling for a moment, then suddenly got up and went to the bathroom. When he came back, he was holding a towel.

"Can't we just put this down?"

"It's not just about getting the sheets dirty ... I don't feel like having sex during my period. There's the smell and cleaning up afterward is a pain too."

"Oh, so you don't want to do it," Jungyu said, nodding. He tossed the towel aside and got back under the covers. "You came because you missed me, right?"

"Of course. You told me you missed me too."

"Yeah, of course I did."

Jungyu quietly turned over to face the wall. She hugged him from behind.

"It feels so nice to finally hug you. I wish we could get married soon and live together, so we could be together every day."

"Yeah, we should get married soon."

Jungyu's voice sounded brittle, like crinkling cellophane.

Come Down to a Lower Place

She stroked his belly and kissed his cheek, feeling a bit deflated by the chill in his voice.

"Are you upset because I didn't want to have sex tonight?"

"No."

"It's just that doing it during my period is uncomfortable. Plus, I think I'm getting a bladder infection, too."

"Again?"

"Yeah, it's not that I don't want to have sex. You know, right?"

"Sure."

Jungyu didn't turn around or hug her back. He kept facing the wall. It wasn't even 11 p.m. yet. She wanted to talk more, but with how things were going, they'd just end up going to bed and heading to work in the morning without resolving anything. She stroked his back, feeling as though she might start crying.

"All right, should we do it?"

After not speaking for almost ten minutes, Jungyu turned around at once.

"Really? But you said it's uncomfortable with your period and the infection. You don't have to if you don't want to."

"It's okay, I want to. We haven't done it for a long time."

"Then I'll grab a towel and some wet wipes. Hang on."

Jungyu quickly picked up the towel he'd tossed aside. He

spread it on the bed and gently lay her down. As he pulled off her sweatpants, she stared up at the ceiling. When he took off her panties, the smell of blood filled the room. He pulled out the wet wipes and carefully wiped her. While he lifted her shirt and licked her nipples, she found herself staring at his bookshelf. *Those comics came out around 2010. I used to really like them. I didn't know Jungyu had them too. Have they always been there?* Even as he put on a condom and entered her, she was skimming the titles on the bookshelf.

After they finished, there was a dark red stain on the beige towel. Jungyu quickly gathered it up and dropped it on the floor. Seul grabbed her panties with the pad still in place and held out her hand.

"The blood will stain if you don't wash it out right away. I need to go to the bathroom anyway. Give it to me."

She tossed the towel into the sink and turned on the cold water, watching as the water turned bright red. The sound of running water masked her peeing. She was relieved it hurt less to urinate than earlier that day. After quickly rinsing out the towel, she tossed it into the laundry basket.

Jungyu was already dressed and was boiling water in the kitchen. "It's late, so tea's better than coffee, right? Chamomile is supposed to help you sleep."

As usual, Jungyu was genuinely happy about Seul's success

at work. He added that he wanted to visit the store once the construction was done, saying they should check out the first floor.

"Is there a jewelry shop? Maybe we could pick out our rings there?"

As soon as Jungyu mentioned ring shopping, Jung Dahan—the employee who'd made that strange comment about blood overflowing—flashed across her mind. How would she react if Seul came to look at rings with Jungyu? Would she wear the same expression as she had tonight? For some reason, she didn't want to bring up Jung Dahan, so instead of replying, she just squeezed his hand.

Jungyu started snoring softly, but even after 1 a.m., Seul couldn't fall asleep. She probably had too much on her mind. On nights like this, trying to force herself to sleep would only mean staring at the ceiling longer. It was better to do something else and let sleep come naturally. Carefully, so as not to wake him, she got up and went to his computer. Maybe watching a movie on Netflix would help.

She randomly picked a movie from Jungyu's long watchlist, but KakaoTalk notifications interrupted her. The app was already open on the computer. As the movie played, the notifications kept sounding. *Who's texting this much at 1 a.m.?* Annoyed, she exited full-screen mode. At the top was a chatroom called "Yummy Ramen" with eighteen unread messages. It was probably a group chat with some friends. Looking at the names, she realized she'd met a few of them before. *I get they're close high school friends, but seriously, texting in the middle of the night when some of us have to work in the morning?* Intending to mute the notifications while watching the movie, she clicked on the chatroom. As soon as she did, one message caught her eye: *But can you even compare it to Jungyu's girlfriend's stinky pussy?*

Her mind went completely white, and for a moment, she couldn't see anything. She started scrolling up, trying to figure out what they had been talking about. The phrase "Jungyu's girlfriend's stinky pussy" was mentioned at least every few days. Sleep was now completely out of the question. She kept scrolling through the chat history. She finally found the first time it came up. It was four months ago.

KO MUNSU.   Hey, isn't Jungyu getting married soon?

OH JUNGYU.   Yeah, man. We're 34 next year.

KIM YONGHWAN.   These days it's totally normal to get married at 34.

Lots of people do it at 40.

KO MUNSU.   Still, when you find someone good, gotta lock it down.

Come Down to a Lower Place

IM JEONGHYEON. Anyone seen Jungyu's girlfriend?

KO MUNSU. Yeah, she's pretty cool. Seems like she's got a good personality and a solid job.

JUNG SEOKCHEOL. But is she hot?

KO MUNSU. Bro, you a child? Still fixating on looks at our age? But yeah, she's cute.

JUNG SEOKCHEOL. Good enough. Not gonna lie, I get pissed every time I fight with my wife cuz I didn't marry her for her looks.

KIM YONGHWAN. LOLOLOLOL

JUNG SEOKCHEOL. But she's gotta have some flaws, right? You better think twice if there's anything.

What seems small now could be divorce material later.

IM JEONGHYEON. Man, you're jinxing him before he's even married.

JUNG SEOKCHEOL. Just spill it. She can't be perfect.

OH JUNGYU. Nobody's perfect. She's got some flaws, yeah.

JUNG SEOKCHEOL. That's what I mean. She clingy or something?

OH JUNGYU. Nah, nothing like that.

JUNG SEOKCHEOL. Then is she a crazy spender?

OH JUNGYU. Hell no. You think I'd marry someone like that?

JUNG SEOKCHEOL. Then what is it? Sex not good?

IM JEONGHYEON.   LMAO

KIM YONGHWAN.   LOLOLOLOLOLOLOL

JUNG SEOKCHEOL.   If that's the case, you gotta really think about it.

OH JUNGYU.   It's not that bad.

KO MUNSU.   Wait, it's really a sex issue?

KIM YONGHWAN.   WTF

JUNG SEOKCHEOL.   What is it? Spill it.

OH JUNGYU.   The sex isn't bad …

It's just … her pussy kinda smells.

KIM YONGHWAN.   OMG. LOLOLOLOL

JUNG SEOKCHEOL.   How bad is it? LOL Does it kill your boner?

IM JEONGHYEON.   NGL sometimes that can be kinda hot.

OH JUNGYU.   If it was like that, I wouldn't complain. It's more like a rotten squid smell from a fridge no one's cleaned for 3 years. Plus there's this weird milky discharge too.

KO MUNSU.   Shit, if it's that bad, she needs to see a doctor. Might get better, maybe bring it down to a grilled squid smell.

KIM YONGHWAN.   Grilled squid? Holy shit! LOLOLOL

Jung Seokcheol: One pump and a sip of beer to go with it, huh?

Come Down to a Lower Place

Seul turned off her computer. Nausea surged through her. She ran to the bathroom and shoved her finger down her throat. She gagged several times, but the squid she'd eaten earlier wouldn't come up. After throwing up the chamomile tea Jungyu had made for her, she vomited twice more, bringing up bright yellow liquid, then stumbled out of the bathroom, exhausted. She was about to crawl into bed when she noticed Jungyu sound asleep with a peaceful expression on his face. He was breathing softly, his mouth slightly open.

She thought of every murder scene she'd seen in movies or shows—smashing someone's head with a brick, strangling a sleeping person, or suffocating them with a pillow. Jungyu would probably twitch and shake. Maybe he'd even hit her, struggling to escape. But in the end, his limbs would go limp, and he'd lose control of his bowels and bladder as the life drained from his body. How awful would that smell be? She gritted her teeth as she stared down at Jungyu, then took a deep breath.

Earlier, Jungyu had said he wanted to see the construction job Seul was overseeing. He was genuinely happy for her and wanted to take their relationship to the next level in the place where she'd achieved that success. She wondered if she should tell him she'd seen the chat. Would he try to make things right? How could she face Jungyu's friends after this?

Lost in thought until 4 a.m., she finally opened an app and called a taxi. She couldn't bear to stay there any longer.

Jungyu didn't wake up as she left, and it wasn't until three hours later that he texted her.

Babe, I thought you were sleeping over. Did you go home?
Yeah, I couldn't sleep.

Out of habit, she reached for her suppository, but anger overwhelmed her, and she threw it against the wall. The applicator and medication scattered everywhere. Grabbing her bag, she stormed out of the house.

Construction typically ran overnight into the morning, sometimes continuing past 10 a.m. The entire floor had to be dug up, with one section requiring even deeper excavation. Removing an entire floor that size wasn't something that could be finished in just a day or two.

One morning, Seul made her way up to the first floor, feeling exhausted. Unlike the basement, the lighting on the first floor was so bright and clear that she found herself staring up at the ceiling. She only snapped out of it when her eyes finally adjusted to the brightness.

Just as she was about to leave, she spotted Jung Dahan. Dahan's smile was as radiant as the sparkling lights, and her paleness was no longer noticeable. She looked genuinely happy, so much so that Seul stopped in her tracks. It was like there was nothing else Dahan would rather be doing than talking to the customer in front of her.

The customer was examining some jewelry on display while holding a pair of earrings. Despite the big smile on her face, Dahan's mouth moved nonstop. Seul wondered what she could be saying. Words from such a radiant face had to be as delightful as the scratch of scented pencil on paper, the feel of soft velvet, or winter sunlight streaming through a window onto a fluffy blanket. Mesmerized, Seul moved closer to Dahan. Brilliant light scattered like falling snow.

"We have other designs too besides the clover," Dahan said, holding a necklace in her palm. "As you can see, the chain is gold, and the hearts on both sides are made of carnelian. It's the same material as the clover you chose earlier. Did you know that Rankip & Adell are famous for their work with carnelian?"

Dahan lifted the necklace and brought a specific part closer for the customer to see.

"Have you heard of cat's eye stone? This one is similar but of a higher grade—it's called tiger's eye, named after the eye of a tiger. Doesn't this look just like a tiger swallowtail in this butterfly design? It almost feels like a real butterfly in a forest, right?"

The customer, with a dazed expression, shifted her gaze to each piece Dahan held up.

"We also have these in the clover design, but as you can see, the color is different. This is made from mother-of-pearl, which forms inside a shell. When you move it like this, see? It creates a rainbow hologram effect."

"How much is this one?"

Dahan handed a piece of paper to the customer. After looking at it for a few seconds, the customer handed it back. "I'll take the necklace too."

While Dahan was completing the sale, another customer approached and began looking at the jewelry. She started speaking hesitantly to Yoon Seonghui, the manager. This customer's voice grew louder as soon as the first customer left.

"I saw this online, so why isn't it here?"

"Ma'am, that product is released every three years in limited quantities. We can't guarantee it'll be in stock when you visit. I'm really sorry."

"Do you sell to people based on how they look? How can you say you don't have it after I've come all this way? Does that make any sense?"

"It's not like that, ma'am."

"What do you mean, 'It's not like that'? I travelled all this way, and now you're telling me I wasted my time?"

Come Down to a Lower Place

Sensing the rising tension, Dahan quickly moved in, stepping closer to the customer. With a warm smile, she spoke softly, as if she were born to put people at ease.

"I'm really sorry. Did you see it on our website?"

"I sure did."

"Then you might have noticed the contact number for our Korea branch …"

"What's that supposed to mean? You just throw a number on the site and expect the customer to handle everything? Miss, is that really how you should be treating people in a luxury store?"

"We don't have the product in stock right now, and I apologize for the inconvenience. But if you leave your contact information, I can notify you as soon as it's available at another store."

"I want to see watches!" the customer demanded, slamming her hand on the display case, drawing attention from nearby shoppers. "Show me another watch then! You must have at least one watch in stock, right?"

In less than five seconds, Dahan presented a new watch to the customer.

"This one is gold with diamond-encrusted sides. It's the best in our essential line."

"Does it have that internal module thing?"

"No, as mentioned, the watches with internal modules are

limited editions. We don't have any in stock right now, but we'll notify you as soon as we find one'…"

The customer snatched the watch box and jabbed it against Dahan's chest.

"Are you kidding me? Do you think I came all this way just to see some random watch? This is a luxury store, right? So why do you only have cheap stuff here? Are you just a temp? Get someone from the head office. Where's the real staff?"

Without missing a beat, Dahan bowed her head.

"I'm very sorry."

Unable to handle the customer's escalating complaints, Seul left the area and headed to the restroom. The restroom on the first floor had a calming effect. Her period was almost over, and her bladder infection was getting better. After urinating a good amount without any burning sensation, Seul came out of the stall and saw the angry customer sitting in front of the powder room mirror, scribbling something on a piece of paper. Annoyed, Seul stood behind her, thinking that if the woman was writing a complaint, she might just "accidentally" spill some water on her.

The woman was jotting down notes in neat handwriting:

SERVICE AND ATTITUDE: Excellent.
UNIFORM CONDITION: Excellent.

Come Down to a Lower Place

PRODUCT EXPLANATION: Excellent.

YOON SEONGHUI: Her makeup doesn't match the brand's concept.

JUNG DAHAN: Tiny bit of grime under the fingernails.

Startled, Seul quickly looked away. She checked her reflection in the mirror, worried the woman might have noticed her reading the note. Luckily, the woman seemed completely uninterested in Seul as she tucked the note into her bag, already stuffed with papers and star markings—probably from visiting other luxury stores. She was likely touring all the brand's stores in Seoul.

As Seul was leaving, she glanced back at Dahan. She felt bad seeing how quickly Dahan had bowed to apologize, even though she hadn't done anything wrong. Would it be too much if she tried to comfort her? After all, they'd only had drinks together once. *But then again, don't we sometimes offer a few kind words to strangers on the bus?* When Seul looked at Dahan's face, it was eerily calm. The cheerful smile had vanished, replaced by a hardened expression. Her eyes were blank, and her facial muscles sagged like she was drained of all energy. She looked as though a shadow of deep cold had fallen over her face. A chill ran down Seul's spine as she quietly walked away.

That evening, just as construction work was about to re-sume, Seul heard a loud argument near the basement entrance. When she went to investigate, she instinctively took a few steps back. It was the old man who had followed her, the one who had chased her all the way to the bus stop, glaring at her while shrieking, "Bin-o-jae!" He scanned the area, then his eyes locked on Seul. His bony hand shot out, grabbing her shoulder. She tried to pull away, but he had no intention of letting go.

"I told you not to do it!"

At his shout, she felt like she was being strangled. She started trembling. Someone stepped between them, but the old man held onto her clothes.

"Please let go of me!"

She shoved him, and he fell to the ground, but he still wouldn't let go. Just as she was about to be pulled down with him, someone grabbed her from behind, and a piece of her work uniform tore away.

"Mister, what's the matter?"

"I told her not to do it! I told her to stop!"

"Team Leader, do you know this man?"

Seul shook her head, trembling. The old man's glare fol-lowed her, sending chills down her spine.

"A while ago, he chased me outside the store, yelling at me to stop the construction … he followed me …"

Come Down to a Lower Place

"He's insane."

"Call the police, quick!"

Someone dialed 9-1-1. Just then, the old man sprang up from the ground and sprinted toward the spot where the crew was digging. He moved so fast for his age that two employees who tried to stop him fell over. The old man dropped to the ground and began scooping up the wet cement, trying to fill the hole with his bare hands. As he clawed at the floor with his nails, his hands quickly became covered in blood. People hesitated to intervene.

"You did call the police, right?" one of them whispered.

"Yeah, they said they'd be here in under ten minutes."

"Sir, we've called the police. Stop causing a disturbance and leave!"

The old man's piercing glare bore into Seul. He lunged at her, grabbing her shoulders with both hands, his fingertips torn and bloody. The employees, who had felt somewhat reassured knowing the police were on their way, panicked and tried to pull the old man off her, but he wouldn't let go. Her mind went blank with terror as his face loomed closer.

"I told you not to do it!" he screamed in her face. "Didn't I warn you? But you women never listen!"

His grip was unbelievably strong. She wondered if his fingers would pierce through her shoulders. Her shoulders felt like they were about to be crushed. Every time the old man shook her, her head bobbed back and forth. Voices shouting her name mixed with the old man's yelling, echoing chaotically in her mind. When people finally managed to separate them, she collapsed on the floor, sobbing.

"Take him away! Take him away right now! Where's the police?"

"Team Leader, we reported him. Oh no ... get her some water!"

Even as two strong men held him down, the old man struggled and screamed. By the time the police arrived, he had thrown himself on the floor, lying flat on his back. He clutched at the remaining bits of cement, grinding his teeth so hard that it was audible. An officer approached Seul and asked if she was okay and if she felt well enough to give a statement about the incident. Even while this was happening, the old man kept repeating, "You have to stop digging! You have to stop!" His shouts were closer to growls. His animal noises seemed to unsettle not only Seul but the officers too, who seemed hesitant to get close.

"You kids don't know a damn thing! You're still wet behind the ears. You have no idea what's buried down here! I bet you've never even heard of Bin-o-jae! Do you even realize what kind of curse you're messing with by digging here?"

Come Down to a Lower Place

When the old man mentioned Bin-o-jae, Seul's hand started to shake again. The officer who was asking her to give a statement took her hand, perhaps sensing her fear. The officer's hand was soft and cool, but it didn't stop Seul's hand from trembling. It felt as if her hand had a mind of its own and was reacting to the word "Bin-o-jae." Even her shoulders started to shake.

"There's a monster down here. It's buried underground and it's made of hatred and bitterness!"

The police tried to pull the old man off the floor, but he clung to whatever was within reach with all his strength. One of the officers knelt beside him, trying to reason with him, but the old man's eerie rage left him speechless.

"You have no idea what you're doing. You're letting Bin-o-jae loose! There's a rotten gutter flowing under here. A rotten gutter you created with your digging is still here! It's been flowing since the Japanese occupation. Since the Japanese occupation!"

"You were probably just born during the Japanese occupation," an officer blurted, unable to hold back. "So what do you know?"

"That's right, I was born during the occupation! Even though I was just a baby, I knew that name. You have no idea what's down here—the stench, the pus, the shapeless mass of vengeful spirits trapped underground! The monster born from between the legs of the women who worked here back when this was the Mitsukoshi Department Store is still alive down here—bitter and reeking like those women's crotches!"

When the officer in charge shook his head, the other officers rushed in to restrain the old man. He flattened himself against the floor like a lizard, letting out a bizarre, inhuman wail. They struggled to raise him, shaking their heads in frustration. One of them looked at the officer in charge, clearly troubled.

"He's too strong!"

"If Bin-o-jae wakes up, if the cursed hole opens again and the primal bitterness, the root of evil, returns, no one will be safe. They should have destroyed this building when they first found it. They should have blown up Mitsukoshi Department Store. When the women who worked here, when their legs swelled up, when they couldn't change their underwear, they should have demolished the whole place! Who brought Bin-o-jae back? Who killed my father?"

Even though old man's words were nonsense, the police exchanged glances with one another at the mention of his father. They'd dealt with plenty of mentally deranged people before, but none as strong as this one. Someone radioed for backup. They needed more officers to tear him off the ground.

Come Down to a Lower Place

"My father lost his mind after opening the lid. He was kicked out of the mental hospital and lived tied up in a corner until he died. His name was Kim Gaebong! I'm Kim Wonsik, the son of Kim Gaebong—the man you all killed!"

"Yes, yes, sir, we understand. We'll listen to everything you want to say, but first, let's go to the station. Do you have any family we can contact?"

While the old man rambled on, Seul was the only one trembling as if she had a fever. Kim Gaebong—the name from the old record, the one who'd lost his mind after removing the floor. Who had written that record, and what had Kim Gaebong seen?

The police officer, noticing Seul's face go pale, draped a blanket over her shoulders. Seul couldn't bring herself to look at the old man, so she kept her head down. As her face moved closer to her lap, she caught a familiar smell.

No, it was more than that. It was similar, but the stench was far more intense. Startled, she looked up. The smell wasn't coming from her.

The entire basement floor was filled with the foul odor. A translucent, mucus seeped up through the ground, wetting the old man's back as he lay on the floor. It spread out beneath him in a circular shape. The source of the stench was clearly this substance. Amid the chaos, the department store's security team came down to assess the situation and immediately pinched their noses.

"Ugh, it's never smelled this bad before."

After asking a few questions, the security team quickly headed back upstairs.

"So, it's just one crazy old man causing trouble? Damn, it stinks!" Even the backup officers were struggling, holding their noses and breathing through their mouths.

"You should have told us to bring gas masks if it was going to be this bad."

"It didn't start smelling like this until just now. Ugh, this is unbearable."

The construction workers and Seul's team were also struggling to stay on their feet because of the stench. The odor brought with it a suffocating humidity, making the dry, freezing winter air outside seem unreal. It was like the smell of sewage or waste, but closer to the smell of sweat, blood, pus, and oozing wounds—the smell of something alive. Only something alive could give off such an overpowering stench, asserting itself so forcefully that it spread its odor into every corner. At first, people just held their noses, but it didn't take long for them to grasp the real nature of the smell. Someone's muttering reached Seul's ears.

"Do you think there something alive down there?"

Come Down to a Lower Place

"Ugh, it smells like squid. Like rotten squid. It's making me want to puke."

"You're right, it does smell like squid."

Even as they held their noses and talked about leaving, the officers tried to lift the old man by his arms and legs. When five strong men grabbed hold of his limbs and head, he couldn't fight them off anymore. Even so, the job was difficult because of his thrashing and kicking. As they forcibly moved him, more mucus oozed out from the ground, and the stench grew even stronger.

"This smell—don't you recognize it? You should know right away where it's from and what it is! You're all cursed. Once you see that horrible thing, none of you will stay sane! Stop now and seal that damned hole. Block it before it spreads! Right now!"

Someone gagged a few times and rushed to the bathroom, covering their mouth, unable to bear the smell any longer. Seul, too, found it almost impossible to endure. Just by coming into contact with the stench, she felt as though her skin was rotting. Breathing through her mouth, she rubbed her hands and arms over her body, as if trying to wipe away the foul odor.

"It's not me, it's that woman you need to arrest! She's the one doing this! I don't know if she's trying to free Bin-o-jae on purpose or just being stupid, but it's not me you need to interrogate, it's that bitch!"

The old man's anger turned back to Seul. Even amidst the stench, people quickly surrounded her, hiding her in the middle of the group, while the police hurriedly recited his rights as they carried the old man away. She could hear bits of legal jargon, like something out of a movie, mentioning the right to remain silent. Although others shielded her from the old man, his shouting still reached her.

"You have no idea what you're doing! Don't ignore the words of an old man! The world is going to be destroyed, I'm telling you, it's going to be destroyed!"

Someone pinched their nose and joked in a nasal voice, "Looks like we need to send him to church on Sunday. He's been watching too much *Mystery Television.*"

The old man was unfazed. He kept raving about doom, the end of the world, and a force that would drive everyone mad. And he didn't forget to curse Seul in between.

"A woman who commits such awful acts will become the host for all vengeful spirits! Every bit of hatred that's built up here since this place was first made will enter your body and destroy you!"

Hearing herself cursed as the "host for all vengeful spirits," Seul turned her head slightly to see the old man through the crowd. He was thrashing around, staring up at the ceiling. Bright red blood streamed from his eyes. One officer, shocked by the sight, momentarily lost his grip on the old man's leg but quickly grabbed it again.

"Listen to me! Everyone involved—everyone in charge and everyone following orders—listen! If it's money you need, I'll give you everything I have! Just, please, stop this! A curse will fall on you, a curse!"

After the old man was dragged away, all that remained was silence and the horrendous smell.

"Oh God, I need some fresh air. Team Leader, you should take a break too. Maybe go upstairs for a bit instead of breathing this in—it'll help clear your head."

One of the police officers standing by Seul helped her up. Leaning on the officer's shoulder, she made her way to the first floor. Without the smell, her mind started to clear.

"Since there was violence involved, it would be best if you came to the station to give your statement."

Seul shuddered. "Does that mean I'll have to see him again? I can't—I'm too scared."

"We'll make sure you don't see him. There are separate areas for giving statements, so don't worry."

As Seul was about to follow the officer, her colleague who'd been standing nearby, taking deep breaths, spoke up.

"Team Leader, I know this isn't the best time to bring it up, but can we really continue the work with that smell? Maybe we should have just poured the concrete and sealed it off like they suggested. Let's rethink our approach and do that now."

At that moment, all Seul could think about was how she'd gone against the orders of the contract—the one that clearly stated they must not dig below the marble under any circumstances. How was she going to explain it? How would she cover the damages? This was the moment she'd dreaded the most. Even at the station while giving her statement, she couldn't stop thinking about the contract. When asked if she was willing to settle with the old man, the contract was the only thing that occupied her mind.

"Just … please make sure he doesn't come near the construction site again. At least until the work is done."

Taking in Seul's dazed expression, the officer looked at her with pity. *Yes, pity me. I'm in more shit than you realize.*

The next day, from early morning, the department store was in chaos. Customers who walked in turned around immediately and fled. By morning, the smell had started to seep into the new wing. The first floor of the main building already reeked so much that no one could step inside. Even those who had been at the construction site the day before couldn't bring themselves to go back in.

Come Down to a Lower Place

In the office of the new wing, General Manager Ha, Manager Kim, and Seul sat facing each other. Seul kept her head bowed like a guilty person. Mr. Ha let out a deep sigh.

"So, are you saying you dug up the floor?"

"Well … we didn't mean to, but yesterday, a crazy old man barged into the construction site, and in the chaos, the floor gave way under him," Seul said, putting the blame on the old man.

Remembering how desperately he had tried to stop the construction, guilt swept over her. *I'm sorry to put this all on you, old man, but you attacked me and cursed at me. I'm not asking for compensation, so please let this slide.*

"Ah … I see. And the old man, did the police take him away?"

"Yes, but I'm not sure if he's still in custody. We agreed to settle the matter on the condition that he stays away from the site, so he probably won't be back."

"I see …"

Mr. Ha buried his head in his hands. Manager Kim, unsure of what to do, watched him nervously. Seul wished she could just disappear right then and there.

Stupid Seul, why couldn't you just follow orders? Instead, you had to insist on digging deeper. If you'd just poured concrete over the old floor, even if the smell came back, it wouldn't have been your fault. Why did you think you could handle a big project like this? You idiot, why do you always mess things up?

She swore a hundred, a thousand times that if she could just get out of this mess, she would never make any big decisions on her own again.

"Um … Mr. Ha, are we going to have to pay damages?"

Without looking up, he said, "But your company didn't dig up the floor. How can we expect Yukwang Construction to pay for it?"

Even though Seul was worried her lie might come out later, she felt a sudden rush of relief. She had narrowly avoided making the company lose money because of her mistake.

"So, does this mean we're continuing with the repairs?"

"Not just continuing—you need to finish as soon as possible. I hope you have a plan. Do you have any idea how much the luxury department pulls in every day? We don't even know what this smell is. What if there's something in the air that corrodes the jewelry? We could lose everything."

"Yes, I understand."

He looked up, his face weary, and stared at Seul. "It might be some kind of acid. If it corrodes pearls … damn."

"Acid?"

"Like hydrochloric or sulfuric acid. Acid, not a base. You know, I heard women are acidic down there. The smell … it's just like that. Oh, but maybe you don't notice it since you're used to your own smell?"

If only I hadn't dug below the marble, I would throw the contract in his face and tell him to go shove it. Seul stared at him, stunned, as he continued in a weary tone.

"This isn't the time to sit around, Team Leader. You need to go back and continue the repairs."

Gritting her teeth, Seul got up and half-ran toward the main building.

She had to rally the workers and somehow get them back down to the basement. Even though they all complained, they grabbed their equipment and headed back down. She urged them to pour the concrete quickly and finish the job in two days. She suggested starting today by sealing off the area they had broken through yesterday as soon as the floor was leveled. But when she got down to the basement, her worst fear had already come true. The entire floor was sticky with slime.

They hadn't expected more slime to come up, so leaving it uncovered yesterday had made things worse. Seul quickly came up with a plan.

"Get the trash pump! Hurry!"

The liquid on the floor was so thick that the pump struggled to suck it up, but after running the machine at full power for three hours, the floor finally became visible. They quickly called in the concrete crew to seal the hole they had uncovered. With the floor cleared, the smell seemed to ease up a bit. But just as they were about to pour the concrete, they noticed something strange. Yesterday, there had been just one hole, but now there were more.

Wearing heavy boots, the concrete worker began pouring into the hole from yesterday, but suddenly, liquid started gushing from a new opening. This time, it was coming out so fast that yesterday's flow seemed like nothing in comparison. The slimy liquid shot out like a fountain, so thick you wouldn't believe it was slime. The awful smell quickly spread throughout the basement again. The concrete worker panicked as the liquid rushed toward him. The slime seemed thicker than ever.

At that moment, Seul noticed a familiar face at the top of the stopped escalator—Jung Dahan. She was looking down at the chaos below, laughing, her head tilted back, with the whites of her eyes glinting above her pupils. Her hair looked brittle and lifeless, and the veins visible beneath her pale skin gave her face a bluish tint. She wore a completely different kind of smile than before. Her features were all in the right places, but somehow, her face looked distorted, as if it were flipped inside out or melting away. It was a smile that seemed to blur the boundaries of her body.

Laughing, Dahan slowly came down to the basement.

Come Down to a Lower Place

A new fear washed over Seul, different from what she'd felt with the old man yesterday. A shiver ran down her spine as she looked up at Dahan. Whether or not she knew Seul was watching, her smile widened as she walked down. Arms spread wide, eyes closed, Dahan took a deep breath, as if she'd been waiting for this horrible stench. As she approached, the liquid on the floor seemed to bubble and boil. People who had come in, puzzled by the stronger smell, froze when they saw Dahan and Seul.

"Is she … a ghost?"

"I don't think so. She's wearing a Saesegae uniform."

Even so, Dahan's expression was terrifying enough to make anyone believe otherwise. The veins on her pale face spread across her body like bruises, and ash began to rise and swirl above the slime. As the ash hit her, Dahan's steps grew heavier. With a chilling smile, she dropped to the slimy floor and started muttering something under her breath.

Having dealt with the old man just the day before, the workers were both exhausted and terrified. A worker who had vomited yesterday ran out, shouting he couldn't take it anymore. Someone stopped another from chasing after him. Amidst the chaos, Dahan, with her pale, bluish face, sat down on the floor, still muttering. It sounded like a chant.

"Greatspiritoffilthaboveandbelowyinandyangsunand-

mooneasttowestautumntospringgovernorofhoursrulerof-
forcesmasterofthenightlordofthefivedirectionsgatherallim-
puritiesherebinojae …"

It was that word again—"Bin-o-jae." Most people didn't
hear what Dahan was chanting, as she was muttering nonstop, but Seul heard it clearly. Dahan repeated "Bin-o-jae"
several times, and each time she did, Seul felt the slimy floor
ripple beneath her.

As the floor rippled, Dahan's voice grew louder until everyone could hear her clearly. She spoke steadily, without
pausing or taking a single breath, but it was obvious she was
calling out to Bin-o-jae. Dahan was summoning Bin-o-jae.

"Comedowncomedownbinojaecomedownwhenthe-
filthofheavenandearthcrumblebinojaecomedownbringsuf-
feringbringstormsbringsorrowandchaoslettheheartsofwom-
enrotinthishumanmessletthepussiesofwomenbetornapartin-
thisstormtheyearswelivedintearsnowtheworldisstainedwith-
filthcomedownbinojaecomedown …"

Her voice sped up, and her hair stood straight up toward
the ceiling. Someone started sobbing in fear. A few people
came to their senses and ran out the door. Seul also wanted
to escape, but she couldn't move. She glanced at the concrete
worker, who was frozen in place, staring at Dahan as she
chanted. She noticed the wet spot spreading between his legs.

Come Down to a Lower Place

The liquid on the floor began to swirl. Pouring more concrete was pointless as the existing layer cracked apart, with chunks breaking off here and there. The liquid surged toward the center of the basement floor. Seul thought she had gotten used to the foul odor, but a stench far more intense than anything she had smelled before filled the air. She had never smelled anything like it. It was a stench that shouldn't exist in this world. She pressed her fingers against her nose, feeling as if the smell might make it bleed. The stench overwhelmed all her senses. The concrete worker fainted, clutching his nose.

From the center of the floor, a massive tentacle rose up like something out of a nightmare. It was just one limb, but it caused the floor to break apart. The entire tentacle couldn't fully emerge. Only the tip of it filled the basement, writhing. Seul stared blankly at what seemed to be a squid's tentacle, feeling as though she were staring into the face of Medusa. She was completely paralyzed.

The tentacle wasn't gray like a squid's. It looked more like a piece of mammalian flesh—massive, red, and covered in slime. Veins crisscrossed its surface, and some of them formed into suckers. It was unmistakably a tentacle, but its skin looked like shredded human flesh. Around the suckers, there were white patches resembling cottage cheese. The slimy liquid on the floor was mixed with clumps of this white discharge. Seul could only think of one thing that looked like this—a vagina with a yeast infection.

Tears of joy streamed down Dahan's face as she staggered to the tentacle and touched it eagerly. The tentacle, as though recognizing its long-time devotee, undulated, rubbing itself against her body. Now covered from head to toe in the tentacle's white secretion, Dahan smiled once again.

"Oh, God of Despair, made from our bodies we have killed, born of our pain and despair, you have finally arrived! Come in, come in, please!"

Seul felt as if her mind and body had completely separated. Though she stood watching Dahan and the tentacle, her eyes didn't seem to belong to her anymore. She couldn't move or look away. Unable to do anything else, she was forced to stand there, witnessing this eerie and unsettling scene. Would she lose her body like this forever? Strangely, the thought didn't make her sad. The smell rising from the floor made it clear that she was a part of this stench, too.

Splat, splat. All around the basement, Seul heard people dropping to the ground. After a concrete worker went down, more people fainted. In a way, they were the lucky ones. One of the equipment workers started laughing hysterically.

"We're all doomed! Corpses have gathered to make a god!

Come Down to a Lower Place

Worship it, worship it! The dead have gathered deep underground!"

As she watched the worker hopping around like a madman, screaming with his eyes rolled back, Seul thought of this so-called Jungbon, who'd had a seizure and was taken to Severance Hospital in 1935, according to the old record. And then there was Kim Gaebong—he went mad three days after digging up the floor, got expelled from the mental hospital, and died chained up. Whatever happened to Jungbon? He must have died long ago. But it didn't matter anymore. Everyone who had managed to stop Bin-o-jae back then was dead, and now it was Seul who had set the course for disaster. She gave a bitter smile. All of a sudden, she pictured a world where everyone lost their minds and merged under the power of Bin-o-jae. This, a vision she'd never had before, came clearly into her mind, yet she didn't find it strange. Of course, it made sense because Bin-o-jae had woken up.

She glanced around and saw that she and Dahan were the only ones looking at Bin-o-jae with clear minds. The others were either sitting on the slimy floor, muttering incoherently while staring up at the ceiling; flopping around like fish out of water; running around, laughing hysterically, only to then roll on the floor and sob; or lying scattered like corpses, whether dead or unconscious. The only ones standing on

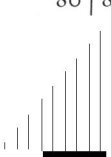

their own two feet were Dahan and Seul … or so she thought, until she noticed someone standing in the corner. It was that old man—Kim Wonsik.

She wasn't afraid of him anymore. Now she knew for certain that Bin-o-jae had invaded her mind. It was Bin-o-jae who had shown her the eerie, beautiful scene of the world being invaded, and it was Bin-o-jae who was calming her, making her accept the situation. Now that Bin-o-jae was inside, it began to manipulate her thoughts. She surrendered completely. She could be wrong, but Bin-o-jae could never be. Bin-o-jae was her despair. It was her death.

And now, Bin-o-jae's words echoed directly in her mind. It wasn't a voice or a smell. Before its message, Seul mentally bowed down.

"I am the great ancient female who lives in the sour, pungent smell of women. They called me It, Bin-o-jae, Disaster, Cthulhu. I built a city of despair in the waters of suffering that women have spilled. Now that I have returned, the voices of vengeful spirits will plunge the world into despair. With tentacles dripping with poison, I will embrace everything and deliver the punishment this world deserves. Your mind will join me in the deep, unknowable darkness, in the embrace of bottomless despair. Together, we will reclaim our world."

As Bin-o-jae spoke, the old man waded through the

thickening slime toward Bin-o-jae's suckers. He bowed to the creature's flesh, showing his reverence. Bin-o-jae's skin contracted sharply. The old man knelt, rubbing his hands together, as if trying to spark a fire, and bowed repeatedly.

"Bin-o-jae, Bin-o-jae. I am Kim Wonsik, descendant of Kim Gaebong, who faced you eighty-four years ago. I grew up hearing stories of you from my father, but he was unworthy to be a proper vessel for you. Cast aside by you, my father went insane, his spirit falling into a hell where he couldn't serve you. Please, accept me into the world of despair you will create. Fill me with your presence."

Seul felt Bin-o-jae's disgust deep within her.

"Bin-o-jae, I don't want to perish like my father. Please, let me play a role in the world you will bring forth."

Bin-o-jae extended a sucker toward the old man. His face lit up as it approached. Numerous suckers sprouted from Bin-o-jae's tentacle as it moved closer, oozing white discharge. The old man wept, kissing the discharge that dripped down.

"Thank you, Bin-o-jae!"

The suckers latched onto the old man's body, dissolving his pants away. His pale, sagging buttocks were fully exposed, and then a sucker attached itself to his genitals. The old man gripped Bin-o-jae's sucker, unable to even scream, thrashing briefly before crumpling to the ground. Dark red blood

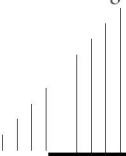

oozed from his genitals as he lay face down in the slime, trembling. Bin-o-jae's message echoed in Seul's mind once more. This time, the same words sprang out of Dahan's mouth. Dahan spoke as Bin-o-jae's mouthpiece, her eyes locked on the old man, the whites gleaming and covered by a slimy film.

"Your father was the same, and so are you. After all this time, you still don't know your place. Did you think you had a part to play in the City of Despair? Knowing you don't, you fought desperately to stop my return. You and your kind have only ever been fuel for endless despair. You will never belong with me."

The old man tried to stand, his body trembling and his voice breaking with anguish.

"I will never … ever let you have your way. I can't … you can't do this. If you won't accept me, you won't get what you want. You won't win!"

The tentacle moved sluggishly, as though indifferent. The old man continued, his bloodshot eyes locked on the bright red tentacle.

"You know exactly how Kim Gaebong lived and died, even if you didn't see it yourself. You trapped him in your illusion. Every day was a nightmare he couldn't escape. His visions were beyond human language, but I grew up hearing about them, so I could understand a little. Even when I was just

Down to a Lower Place

learning to speak, he would talk about Bin-o-jae in a language that wasn't human. Once, I was so terrified I couldn't eat or sleep for two days and could only cry. Everyone thought my father was insane, and he spent his days locked in a corner, barely eating, barely shitting. He couldn't use the bathroom, couldn't speak like a normal person. He was stuck in a world of despair and vengeful spirits, Bin-o-jae's world, where there was no difference between day and night, freezing cold or boiling heat. You know what it's like to live in that world without ever truly being a part of it. My father wanted to die but couldn't. Eventually, they shackled his ankles because he was a disgrace to the family, and my mother had to clean up after him every day. When I was sixteen, he finally died, and even then, he couldn't bear to close his eyes."

Suddenly, the old man stood up. He grabbed a metal crowbar that was nearby and swung it at the back of Dahan's head. Her eyes rolled back. Blood spurted from her head as she crumpled forward, foaming at the mouth, unable to speak. As if that wasn't enough, he began stomping on her body. The tentacle connected to Dahan flinched and recoiled, turning pale as if it had lost its blood supply, and dropped limply to the ground. Bin-o-jae's power was weakening.

Seul instinctively rushed over and shoved the old man. He fell to the ground, and she lifted Dahan, propping her against a pillar. The old man raised the crowbar again and charged at Seul.

"I will never die like my father! Even if the world ends, that's not going to happen!"

The now pale tentacle of Bin-o-jae wrapped around Seul's legs and yanked her with surprising speed. The old man's crowbar missed her, striking the floor. As she was dragged across the slimy floor through the stench, she twisted her body in the opposite direction. In that moment, she saw Bin-o-jae's eye.

The glowing yellow eye of Bin-o-jae was enormous, large enough to fill her entire world. Within it were all the grudges of the old Mitsukoshi Department Store, the stubbornness forged by those grudges, the sorrow that had seeped through the cracked bricks, the despair of those who had suffered humiliation there, their ruined backs and knees, the stench of rotting vaginas and blood-stained underwear, and all the broken women, their hearts torn apart by shame and filth. And deeper still, there was something vast, terrible, unspeakable.

Bin-o-jae stared at Seul with its yellow eye, wrapping her tightly in its tentacle. White discharge gushed over her like foam. Seeing Seul trapped in the white fluid, the old man charged at Bin-o-jae's eye with his crowbar. But Bin-o-jae quickly formed a barrier, like a film, to block him, and the crowbar bounced off.

Down to a Lower Place

Inside Bin-o-jae's barrier, she felt the suckers gently latch onto different parts of her body. She wondered if this was what it felt like to be back inside her mother's womb. As Bin-o-jae's body merged with hers, the stench faded, becoming distant. Now the old man's shrieks were barely audible. The suckers embraced Seul gently, filling her with a world of pain. Without the need for human words, Bin-o-jae's language became even more complete.

Bin-o-jae wasn't its only name. Long ago, it had been called Cthulhu, but even that wasn't its real name. Squirming beneath the basement floor, it grew larger and more complex. Only within its embrace did Seul finally grasp what it really was. Every sucker on Bin-o-jae was a living entity of its own. Every part of its body was different, yet they were all one. There were no conflicting judgments because Bin-o-jae didn't judge. Bin-o-jae was simply warm despair, a single entity of stickiness.

Each sucker held a different memory from ancient times to Dahan's own experiences. Seul felt her own memories being absorbed as well: Jungyu encroaching on her body, the mockery she faced over the smell of her vagina, the long, painful menstrual cramps. She also felt the pain of others, as though she were being stabbed with a needle. Blood that wouldn't clot flowed through Bin-o-jae. She felt the chafed groins of the girls from the Mitsukoshi Department Store, unable to change their pads, as well as the chafing of Dahan and her colleagues, their knees twisting under bright lights, as they waited for a chance to go to the bathroom.

Despite the pain she felt throughout her body, Seul strangely felt at peace. The white discharge swirling around Bin-o-jae never stopped, never cooled. New memories constantly flowed downward, like water, like violence, like excretions. Bin-o-jae absorbed all those painful memories and grew. Since the beginning of time, Bin-o-jae had never shrunk. And just like Bin-o-jae, Seul's body became sticky too.

As the suckers latched onto different parts of her body, she suddenly thought of sex with Jungyu. She used to love the clean, fluffy blanket on his bed. No matter what pain she faced outside, she felt as though she could forget everything under that blanket. It was a cozy, protective bunker, separating her from the world. She'd tried to forget many things under that blanket, but in reality, nothing was ever truly forgotten.

Bin-o-jae's embrace was the opposite of Jungyu's blanket. It was damp and sticky. Pain flooded in, more intense than she had ever known. As she fully surrendered to it, she realized once again that there was no escape. Oddly enough, she didn't feel anxious about the pain that was already there. In the humid air, as she touched the foul discharge, she realized she was now connected to all the memories that made up Bin-o-jae. She kept reassuring herself despite the discomfort and distress. When she finally found some relief, every part of Bin-o-jae seemed to relax and rejoice with her. They shared the pain, yet felt a sense of peace. She didn't resist as the discharge seeped into her eyes. Through her blurry vision, she looked past Bin-o-jae's barrier and saw someone behind the crying old man—a boy, strangely familiar.

He was trembling, pointing something at Bin-o-jae. She squinted and then felt a jolt of shock as she realized she had to warn Bin-o-jae. But just as she grabbed onto its suckers, taser darts flew. The barrier shattered, and without its protection, she was thrown to the floor. The slime that was pooled on the ground vanished without a trace. Bin-o-jae hardened, unable to even close its eye, and its tentacle dropped limply to the floor. Seul, trembling like a child lost in a strange place, reached out and managed to grasp the hardened tip of the tentacle. When she looked up, she saw Minhwan, the temp worker. He wore the same vest he'd had on when he escorted her to the staff restrooms. Trembling and crying, he locked his gaze on Bin-o-jae's bright yellow eye as he sank to the floor.

"I told them I didn't want to go in … but they said my contract renewal was coming up, that I should just get it done … th-that …"

He covered his face with his hands, still holding the taser.

The old man took the taser from Minhwan and fired it again at the now still Bin-o-jae. The creature blinked its yellow eye, then released a powerful surge of energy that struck the old man and Minhwan before vanishing. All that remained was a gaping hole where Bin-o-jae had been. Minhwan, who'd been struck, started punching himself repeatedly in the face. The old man grabbed Minhwan's hands tightly.

"Did you see it?"

Minhwan shrieked in a language no one had ever heard, occasionally mixing in human words.

"Curse … destruction … no, no … go in and get the contract renewal … why me … vacation … home … the end … Mom … no no!"

The old man shook his head, watching Minhwan babble incoherently. Then, with a bitter smile, he began to weep.

"You're like the rest of us now. You'll walk the same hellish path. I'm done for too. You're young and defenseless, so you went down quickly. But I'm finished. The only way to survive now, the only chance we've got, is to make sure Bin-o-jae never comes back. But how I'll go on …"

He clung to Minhwan, crying with him. Bin-o-jae's message, which it had left before disappearing, kept echoing in Seul's mind. Minhwan, who had been speaking in the language of beasts and the dead, collapsed, writhing grotesquely on the floor. The old man slapped himself hard. He felt the spot where Bin-o-jae had vanished and frantically brought over a bucket of concrete.

"It's no use. We failed again, it's all over for you. We need to seal the floor so it can't come back."

Seul wanted to tell him not to dump the concrete so recklessly, but she had no strength left. She could only lie there on the floor and watch the old man thrash around. Dahan, who had fallen earlier with blood streaming from her head, got up and stared blankly at the place where Bin-o-jae had been.

A wail erupted from Dahan. She crawled across the floor to where Bin-o-jae had vanished and began clawing at the ground. The wet concrete was dug up again as the old man kicked her frantically, but Dahan kept reaching for the floor, her hands moving desperately, even under his assault.

"How can this happen again? How, after everything we've endured for so long, how could this happen?"

Dahan's voice merged with Bin-o-jae's, her body shuddering as she slapped the old man across the face with a concrete-covered hand, sending him crashing into a pillar.

"Bleeding every time I piss, losing the space inside my body piece by piece, standing like a stone statue because I have to keep smiling, breaking down in a body that's no longer human. After all that … how could this happen again?"

There was blood in her voice. Seul couldn't see it, but she could feel it and smell it. She felt Dahan's bitterness deep within her. A chill ran down her spine, making her hands shake. After striking the old man, Dahan started scooping up the scattered concrete with her bare hands. Her strength didn't seem her own. The speed with which she cleared the concrete was unnatural. Seul remembered the old man rushing toward her with unbelievable speed when they first met. She recalled the terror that made her run without knowing why. The cursed Kim Gaebong; Kim Wonsik, who inherited the eyes that saw the bottom of the world; the speed and power of Bin-o-jae … Kim Wonsik, who had begged Bin-o-jae to possess him … Even though Seul had no strength left, she reached out. Her movements grew faster. Bin-o-jae's power had seeped into her too.

Meanwhile, the old man picked up the crowbar again and swung it at Dahan's head as she continued digging. This time was different from the first. The sharp end of the crowbar drove straight into her temple. Dahan opened her mouth wide, gasped for breath, then slowly collapsed to the side.

Come Down to a Lower Place

Blood spurted up as the light drained from her wide-open eyes. The old man shoved her limp body aside with his foot, resumed gathering the concrete, pushed it into the hole, and began to cry. He sobbed like a child, sitting on the ground. Blood from Dahan's head poured into the gaping hole.

"It's all over. Everything's over now. I'll go insane too. I'll end up just like my father, tied up in a mental hospital, dying with my mouth sealed shut."

When Seul met the old man's blank stare, his sobbing grew even more pitiful.

"Do you know what my father saw? Every single day, he saw it. They threw him out of the mental hospital because he couldn't stop talking about it. Even when he was locked in his room, he saw it. Out in the fields, he saw it. But the most terrifying part? He saw it clearest in my mother's pussy. My father's mouth was a filthy pit of hell. No one wanted to hear the things he said, so they sealed his mouth shut. Only I, just a kid, sometimes set him free and found the eyes looking out from that pit. Every day, he begged for death, but he couldn't choose it, with Bin-o-jae's world waiting for him on the other side. I've kept my sanity until now because I shared only half of my father's world, but now it's over. Now that I've seen what my father saw, there is no way to escape Bin-o-jae. The only way to avoid it, the thing I fear the most, *is* to fully enter Bin-o-jae's world."

The old man, still sobbing, moved toward Seul. She reached out as quickly as she could, but he grabbed her hand. Slowly, he whispered into her ear. And into her ear, he whispered it. She heard a distant scream and then fainted.

Seul was rescued by the police two days later. They treated the incident as a stalking case involving Kim Wonsik, who had mental health issues. Seul told them she could barely remember anything.

A new manager ended up taking over the construction project in Seul's place, and the decision was made to dig deeper into the floor. Oddly, Saesegae Department Store didn't demand any compensation for damages. Seul went on leave for health reasons while the situation was being sorted out. She was considered a victim in every aspect. She learned that Kim Wonsik had seen his ominous predictions through. The officer who had first taken her statement after the incident shared the details with her.

"He can barely speak. Every time he opens his mouth, he spews such horrifying things that they had to gag him at the hospital. And that young security guard, he shot himself with a taser and died right there on the spot. No one knows where he got it—not the security company, not Saesegae."

The officer, who had just shared the grim news about Kim

Wonsik and Minhwan, looked troubled. A flash of regret crossed her face, as if she realized she'd said too much.

"Oh, I'm sorry ... you probably didn't want to hear that."

Seul smiled and shook her head. She opened her bag and saw the wedding invitations she had left over after handing them out the day before. She pulled one out and handed it to the officer.

"Officer, you've worked so hard. You don't need to bring a wedding gift—just stop by if you have time and enjoy the buffet."

"Oh, you're getting married? Wow, congratulations!"

Seul lowered her head shyly, feeling a slight itch on her inner thigh.

As soon as they parked in front of the shop, Jungyu quickly got out of the car. Before Seul had even unbuckled her seatbelt, he was already opening her door. These days, Jungyu seemed to be in an especially good mood, and why wouldn't he be? He was about to marry the woman he loved. She thought it was a good thing to marry a man so eager to be with her. She stepped out of the car as he held the door open.

She'd already picked out four dresses for the photoshoot and one for the wedding ceremony. Invitations had gone out, and things were moving quickly. Maybe that's why, despite being happy, Jungyu seemed anxious, almost impatient. He hurriedly opened the shop door and called out Seul's name. They say the bride is the star of the wedding, so that was probably why everything was booked under her name.

"What the bride wants matters the most. You have such pretty shoulders—a bell-line dress would look great on you. And with your slim figure, a mermaid dress would really suit you, too."

Jungyu walked over, holding up a mermaid dress. "You'd look like a total celebrity in this. Can you try it on?"

"Let's keep looking. I'm not really comfortable with tight dresses."

"But come on, it's a once-in-a-lifetime moment! You'd look amazing in something like this."

Seul looked away and turned to the shop assistant. "Do you have any dresses that don't drag on the ground?"

"You mean for the photos?"

"Oh, so people don't often wear ankle-length dresses for the ceremony?"

"Well, most brides prefer longer, more elegant dresses for the ceremony—like the one the groom picked earlier. But for photos, ankle-length dresses are popular. Would you like to see some? They're over here."

Come Down to a Lower Place

Seul leaned in and whispered to Jungyu. "I just want something I can walk in by myself."

"I don't know ... You think our families would be okay with a shorter dress?"

"Our families?"

"Well, if you're happy, I'm okay with it, I guess. I'm just worried they might say something."

"Oh ... okay."

Seul ran her hand over the dresses, but her mind drifted back to work. No one blamed her for anything related to Kim Wonsik. Instead, they'd comforted her, feeling sorry for her—running into a crazy old man and suffering so much because of it. She hadn't lost her position as a team leader, but lately, it felt like the important deals were passing her by. Two of her colleagues had quit. One had quit right after the Saesegae incident, and she'd heard he'd asked for a transfer to another team only to be denied. Rumors about the incident spread quickly. The people who told her to ignore the gossip clearly had their own reasons for bringing it up, and Seul understood why. Deep down, they blamed her. When she announced her wedding, everyone had congratulated her, but she sensed the truth behind their smiles. Her team members did seem genuinely happy for her, yet suddenly, Seul found herself wondering if Yoon Seonghui, Jung Dahan's former boss, had managed to keep her position.

Seul stepped into the fitting room, carrying both an ankle-length dress and a mermaid dress. As she undressed and hung up her clothes, she thought how this moment felt like a scene straight out of a movie or show—the bride trying on a beautiful wedding dress while her soon-to-be husband stands up, applauding and praising her beauty. It was the same scene in every romance.

Once an ugly duckling, the heroine spreads her wings like a beautiful swan under the bright lights. The hero at her side cheers at her transformation. Sure, he loves her for who she is on the inside, but a magical transformation is always necessary. Ever since *that* day, whenever Seul saw romantic scenes like that, she felt Dahan's pale face staring back at her. She knew all too well that Dahan's gaunt face now lived inside her.

As she pulled off her pants, "it" poked its head out as usual. She'd known from the itching earlier that this was the cause. A strong whiff from her vagina hit her, but instead of frowning, she gently pressed "it" down. Today, for some reason, it resisted more than usual, showing no intention of going back in. She smiled softly and pulled the dress over her head. Only when she felt the tightness around her waist did she realize she'd put on the mermaid dress Jungyu had picked earlier. *Wow, I'm really out of it today.* From outside, she heard the employee's voice.

Come Down to a Lower Place

"Do you need help with the dress?"

Seul parted the curtain slightly, and the employee quickly stepped in, adjusting her here and there before zipping her up. After using a few pins to perfect the waistline, she gasped, marveling at how beautiful Seul looked. A bright, genuine smile spread across her face. It was a smile Seul had seen so many times before. Even today, she'd seen the same smile on the faces of strangers at least three times. Seul smiled back.

When she drew back the curtain and stepped out, Jungyu exclaimed in admiration as if he'd been waiting. As always, he was polite and sweet.

"Wow … I'm speechless. You look amazing. Just thinking about you walking down the aisle in that is getting me excited already."

Jungyu touched her waist lightly, his expression dreamy as he laughed. The itch on her inner thigh grew worse. Seul discreetly reached down to feel her crotch through the dress. "It" was sticking out now, enough to be felt through the fabric—a round, bulging sucker. As the dress brushed against it, the sucker eagerly latched on, pulling the fabric in. *No, I can't have it showing like this. Not now.* She tried to placate it in her mind, pressing down a bit harder, and it finally disappeared.

"What is it? Is something wrong?"

Seeing Jungyu's worry, Seul shook her head. His

KakaoTalk chat was open on his phone, but she didn't care anymore. Instead of sticking out, the suckers inside her body were pulling from within. There was a strange sensation—a mix of calm and pain. Without realizing it, Seul glanced at Jungyu's crotch. It wasn't her doing; it was the suckers. They were hungry, feeding her all sorts of painful memories. She soothed them quietly. *Just a little longer, just a little more.* Feeling the comforting pain, Seul returned to the fitting room to try on the second dress. Jungyu probably wouldn't be as excited about this one.

As she unzipped the dress, Seul whispered, "Don't worry, just a little longer, Bin-o-jae. Before long, I'll fully welcome you inside me—and the destruction to come."

Suddenly, Bin-o-jae's sucker spewed a thick, white discharge from her vagina.

Come Down to a Lower Place

honfordstar.com